D1307439

LET'S READ
AV²
BY WEIGL™
ADDED VALUE • AUDIO VISUAL

Go to **www.av2books.com**, and enter this book's unique code.

BOOK CODE

L541488

AV² by Weigl brings you media enhanced books that support active learning.

AV² provides enriched content that supplements and complements this book. Weigl's AV² books strive to create inspired learning and engage young minds in a total learning experience.

Your AV² Media Enhanced books come alive with...

Audio
Listen to sections of the book read aloud.

Video
Watch informative video clips.

Embedded Weblinks
Gain additional information for research.

Try This!
Complete activities and hands-on experiments.

Key Words
Study vocabulary, and complete a matching word activity.

Quizzes
Test your knowledge.

Slide Show
View images and captions, and prepare a presentation.

... and much, much more!

Published by AV² by Weigl
350 5th Avenue, 59th Floor
New York, NY 10118

Website: www.av2books.com   www.weigl.com

Copyright ©2014 AV² by Weigl
All rights reserved. No part of this publication may be reproduced, stored in a retrieval system, or transmitted in any form or by any means, electronic, mechanical, photocopying, recording, or otherwise, without the prior written permission of the publisher.

Library of Congress Control Number: 2013934644
ISBN 978-1-62127-494-0 (hardcover)
ISBN 978-1-62127-500-8 (softcover)

Printed in the United States of America in North Mankato, Minnesota
3 4 5 6 7 8 9 0 17 16 15 14

032014
WEP060314

Senior Editor: Aaron Carr
Art Director: Terry Paulhus

Weigl acknowledges Getty Images as the primary image supplier for this title.

Summer

Science Kids
Seasons

CONTENTS

There are four seasons in a year.
Summer is one of the seasons.
Summer is the warmest season
of the year.

4

Spring

Summer

Summer comes after spring and before fall.

Winter

Fall

Summer comes when the Earth faces toward the Sun.
This means more heat from the Sun gets to the Earth.

6

Days are longer in the summer than they are in other seasons. The first day of summer is the longest day of the year.

9

Summer days are very long near the North and South Poles. The Sun may only go down for a few hours each day.

The hottest days of summer
are sometimes called dog days.
A bright star rises with the Sun
in July and early August.
This star is called the dog star.

The dog star is part of a group of stars
that make the shape of a dog.
It is the brightest star in the group.

13

14

The extra sunlight during summer helps plants grow.
This is because plants use sunlight to make their food.

Baby animals grow and play
in the summer.
They learn how to find food
and stay safe.

16

Some animals dig into the ground
in very hot places.
This helps them keep cool.

Farmers grow their crops
in the summer.
They water the crops
to help them grow.

20

Summer Quiz

Test what you have learned about summer. Summer is the warmest season of the year. What signs of warm weather do you see in these pictures?

23

KEY WORDS

Research has shown that as much as 65 percent of all written material published in English is made up of 300 words. These 300 words cannot be taught using pictures or learned by sounding them out. They must be recognized by sight. This book contains 71 common sight words to help young readers improve their reading fluency and comprehension. This book also teaches young readers several important content words, such as proper nouns. These words are paired with pictures to aid in learning and improve understanding.

Page	Sight Words First Appearance	Page	Content Words First Appearance
4	a, are, four, in, is, of, one, the, there, year	4	seasons, summer
5	after, and, before, comes	5	fall, spring, winter
6	Earth, faces, from, gets, means, more, this, to, when	6	heat, Sun
9	days, first, other, than, they	10	hours, North and South Poles
10	down, each, few, for, go, long, may, near, only, very	12	August, dog, July, shape, star
12	group, it, make, part, sometimes, that, with	15	sunlight
15	because, food, grow, helps, plants, their, use	18	ground
16	animals, find, how, learn, play	20	crops, farmers
18	into, keep, places, some, them	22	quiz, signs
20	water		
22	about, do, have, pictures, see, these, what, you		

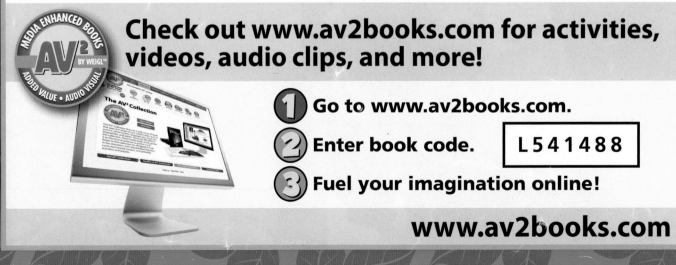

Check out www.av2books.com for activities, videos, audio clips, and more!

1 Go to www.av2books.com.

2 Enter book code. L 5 4 1 4 8 8

3 Fuel your imagination online!

www.av2books.com